RS✦M

MARGARET RIZZA

Mass of Saint Benedict
a musical setting for Common Worship

The Royal School of Church Music, 19 The Close, Salisbury, Wiltshire, SP1 2EB

RS✦M

The Royal School of Church Music
19 The Close, Salisbury, Wilts, SP1 2EB
Tel: +44 (0)1722 424848   Fax: +44 (0)1722 424849
E-mail: press@rscm.com Website: www.rscm.com
Registered charity 312828

Distributed exclusively in North America by GIA Publications, Inc.
7404 S. Mason Ave., Chicago, IL 60638
Toll free: 800 442 1358 Website: www.giamusic.com

Mass of Saint Benedict

a musical setting for Common Worship
by
Margaret Rizza

First published 2011

Cover image: Plaque with Image of St. Benedict (enamel & copper), French School, (13th century) /
© Czartoryski Museum, Cracow, Poland / The Bridgeman Art Library

RSCM Catalogue Number: RC188
Order number: C0864
ISBN: 978-0-85402-191-8

Music setting by Donald Thomson
Printed in Great Britain by Caligraving Ltd, Thetford

FOREWORD

For many years Saint Benedict has been, for me, a source of inspiration. His famous Rule written fifteen hundred years ago has much to tell us in our noisy, highly technological and materialistic twenty-first century.

The Benedictine way, which is timeless, is founded upon three basic principles: prayer, sacred scripture (Lectio Divina) and work. Enshrined in these three principles is a way of life embracing humility, stability, obedience, discipline, stewardship and vocation – all issues of paramount importance which face us today.

Benedictine spirituality offers more a way of life, an attitude of mind rather than a set of religious rules. It is rooted in scripture and is part of the wisdom tradition of Christianity dealing with the very purpose and meaning of life. It embraces living out one's daily life lived in and through Christ.

I follow a contemporary commentary, of which there are many excellent ones, as I struggle very much with the actual words of the Rule itself. I find it gives me a framework and grounds my life in essential values living as I do today in such a challenging world.

Saint Benedict writes with tremendous simplicity and an awareness of the 'ordinary'. I have been guided therefore by this openness of simplicity and consequently the music I have written is simple. It is important that it can be sung easily by congregations as well as by choirs who can lift up their voices in praise, worship, thanksgiving, reconciliation, joy and love – a community held together by praying through music.

This Mass is dedicated with gratitude to Saint Benedict.

I do want to thank Donald Thomson for the skilful music setting and editing of this Mass. You were always there to make changes, adding and subtracting where necessary, and giving so much time, patience and good humour during these months of work.

To Tim Ruffer a very special 'thank you' for all the help, encouragement and advice you have never failed to give me. I have felt so supported by this partnership which has contributed greatly to the writing of the music. It is also a great privilege to be published by the Royal School of Church Music, an organization for which I have so much respect and admiration.

Margaret Rizza
Sevenoaks
21st March 2011

Kyrie

Words: from Common Worship Order One

Music: Margaret Rizza

CANTOR or SATB CHOIR or ORGAN SOLO

Christ, _____ have mer - cy.

CONGREGATION

Christ, _____ have mer - cy.

CHOIR unison

Christ, _____ have mer - cy.

coll' 8 (if played on piano)

6

CANTOR or SATB CHOIR or ORGAN SOLO

Lord, have mer - cy.

CONGREGATION

Lord, have mer - cy.

CHOIR unison

Lord, have mer - cy.

coll' 8 (if played on piano)

Gloria in excelsis

Words: from Common Worship Order One

Music: Margaret Rizza

peace to his peo - ple, peace to his peo - ple on earth.

peace to his peo - ple, peace to his peo - ple on earth.

CONGREGATION *f*

Lord God, hea - ven - ly King, al - migh - ty God and

CHOIR *f*

Lord God, hea - ven - ly King, al - migh - ty God and

Fa – ther, we wor-ship you, we give you thanks, we praise you for your glo – ry.

Fa – ther, we wor-ship you, we give you thanks, we praise you for your glo – ry.

Lord God, hea-ven-ly King, al-migh – ty God and Fa – ther, we

Lord God, hea-ven-ly King, al-migh – ty God and Fa – ther, we

10

worship you, we give you thanks, we praise you for your glory.

Meno mosso ♩ = c.60-66

CONGREGATION (Optional to bar 52)

Lord Je-sus Christ, on-ly Son of the Fa-ther, Lord God,

CHOIR

Lord Je-sus Christ, on-ly Son of the Fa-ther, Lord God,

Lamb of God, you take a-way the sin of the world: have

Lamb of God, you take a-way the sin of the world: have

41

mer - cy, have mer - cy on us;

mer - cy, have mer - cy on us;

a tempo

44

CONGREGATION *mf*

you are seat-ed at the right hand of the Fa - ther: re-

CHOIR *mf*

you are seat-ed at the right hand of the Fa - ther: re-

mf

a tempo

mf

ceive___ our___ prayer, re - ceive our___ prayer.

MELODY INSTRUMENT (Optional)

mf

ceive___ our___ prayer, re - ceive our___ prayer.

mf

un poco rit.

CONGREGATION

f

For

CHOIR: Optional WOMEN only

f

For

f

un poco rit.

14

you a-lone are the Ho – ly One, you__ a-lone are the Lord,

you a-lone are the Ho – ly One, you__ a-lone are the Lord,

you a-lone are the Most__ High, you__ a-lone are the Most High,

CHOIR: Optional MEN only

you a-lone are the Most__ High, you__ a-lone are the Most High,

Tempo Primo ♩. = c.72-76

61
CONGREGATION
Je - sus Christ, with the Ho - ly
CHOIR
Je - sus Christ, with the Ho - ly
66
poco rit.
f
Spi - rit, Je - sus Christ, with the Ho - ly Spi - rit, in the
S. SEMI-CHORUS/MELODY INST.
in the
Spi - rit, Je - sus Christ, with the Ho - ly Spi - rit, in the
poco rit.

71
a tempo
glo - ry, the glo - ry of God the Fa - ther, in the
glo - ry, the glo - ry of God the Fa - ther, in the
glo - ry, the glo - ry of God the Fa - ther, in the
a tempo
f
75
glo - ry, the glo - ry of God the Fa - ther.
glo - ry, the glo - ry of God the Fa - ther.
glo - ry, the glo - ry of God the Fa - ther.
cresc.
2

79
ff
A – men, a – men,
ff
A – men, a – men,
ff
A – men, a – men,
ff
ff
83
molto cresc. e rit. al fine
a – – men, a – – men.
(Optional upper part)
a, a – – men.
molto cresc. e rit. al fine
a – – men, a – – men.
molto cresc. e rit. al fine

Gospel Acclamation

Words: from Common Worship Order One

Music: Margaret Rizza

Con spirito ♩. = 88

MELODY INSTRUMENT (Optional)

If a shorter introduction is required,
start in bar 3

Ped.

CELLO (Optional)

CONGREGATION

Al - le - lu - ia, al - le - lu - ia,

CHOIR

S.
A.

Al - le - lu - ia, al - le - lu - ia,

T.
B.

al - le - lu - ia, al - le - lu - ia.

al - le - lu - ia, al - le - lu - ia.

Quasi recitativo

CANTOR *mf*

Example verse: May the Fa-ther of our Lord Je-sus Christ en - ligh-ten the eyes of our mind,

mf

For extended ending with Descant cut to

so that we can see what hope his call holds for us.

rit.

rit.

Simple ending

Tempo I

CONGREGATION

Al - le - lu - ia, al - le - lu - ia,

CHOIR

Al - le - lu - ia, al - le - lu - ia,

S.
A.

T.
B.

Tempo I

al - le - lu - ia, al - le - lu - ia.

al - le - lu - ia, al - le - lu - ia.

rall.

rall.

Extended ending with Descant

Tempo I

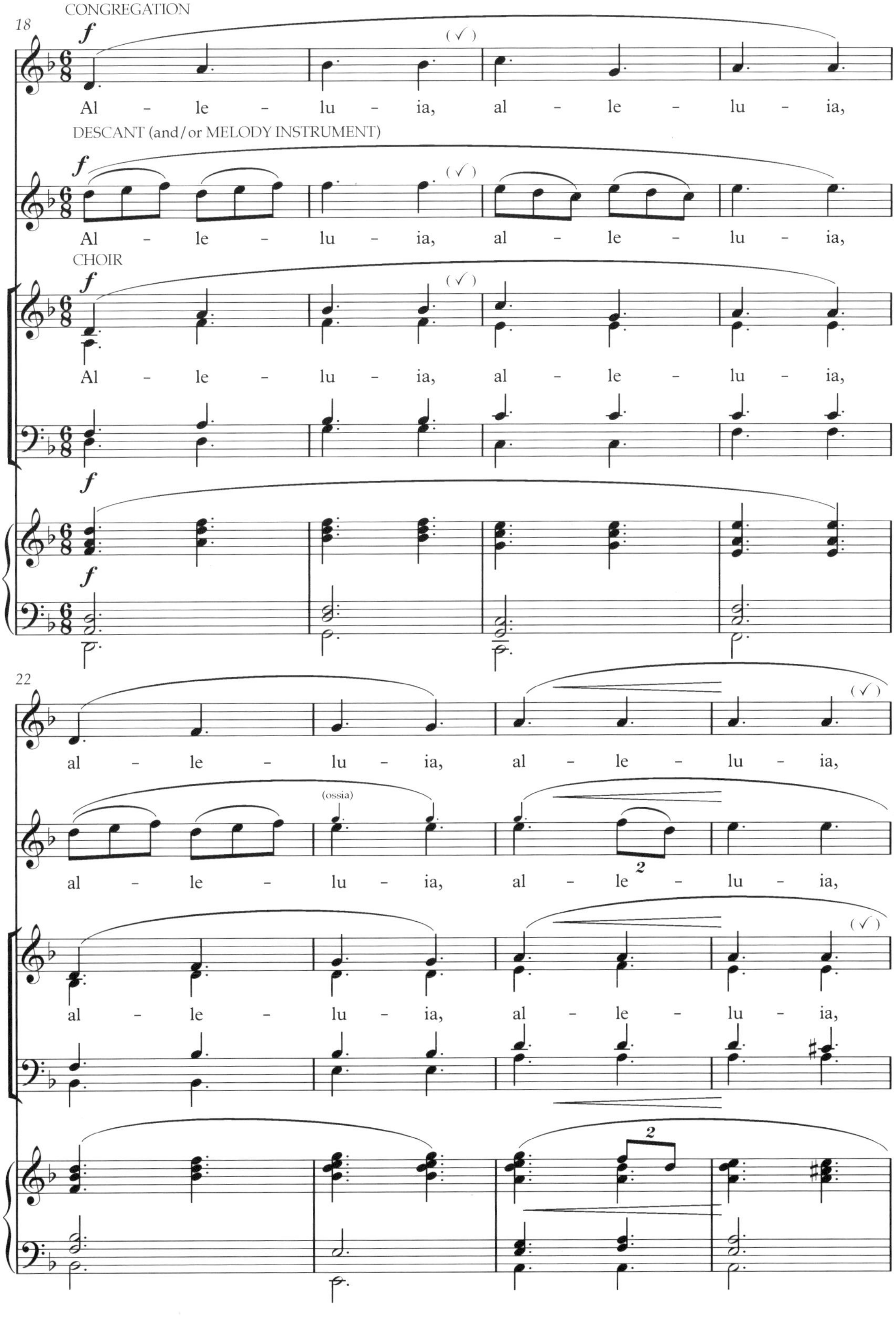

molto rit. e cresc. al fine
26
al - le - lu - ia, al - le - lu - ia.
al - le - lu - ia, al - le - lu - ia.
al - le - lu - ia, al - le - lu - ia.
molto rit. e cresc. al fine

Sanctus and Benedictus

Words: from Common Worship Order One

Music: Margaret Rizza

Largo, very flexible ♪ = 116

MELODY INSTRUMENT (Optional)

mp

Ped.
CELLO (Optional)

CONGREGATION

Ho-ly, ho-ly, ho-ly Lord, God of power and might,

CHOIR unison

S.
A.

Ho-ly, ho-ly, ho-ly Lord, God of power and might,

T.
B.

Ho - ly, ho - ly, ho - ly Lord, God of power and might,

Ho - ly, ho - ly, ho - ly Lord, God of power and might,

CONGREGATION

Hea - ven and earth are full of your glo - ry, are full of your glo - ry.

CHOIR

Hea - ven and earth are full of your glo - ry, are full of your glo - ry.

Ho - san - na, ho - san - na, ho -
Ho - san - na, ho - san-na in the high-est. Ho -
Ho - san - na, ho - san - na, ho -

Largamente

san - na in the high - est. Ho - san - na, ho - san - na in the
san - na in the high - est.
san - na in the high - est. Ho - san - na, ho - san - na in the

26
Tempo I
CONGREGATION
mp
high - est.
Bles - sed is he who comes, who
CHOIR: Optional WOMEN only
mp
high - est.
Bles - sed is he who comes, who
mp
Tempo I
mp
31
comes in the name of the Lord.
Bles - sed is he who comes, who
CHOIR: Optional MEN only
comes in the name of the Lord.
Bles - sed is he who comes, who

SOPRANOS DESCANT or MELODY INSTRUMENT (Optional)

comes in the name of the Lord. Ho - san - na, ho -

Ho - san - na, ho -

Ho - san - na, ho -

comes in the name of the Lord. Ho - san - na, ho -

Largamente   molto rit.

san - na, ho - san - na in the high - est. Ho - san - na, ho -

san - na, ho - san - na in the high - est. Ho - san - na, ho -

san-na in the high-est. Ho - san - na in the high - est.

san - na, ho - san - na in the high - est. Ho - san - na, ho-

Largamente   molto rit.

43
rall. al fine
san - na in the high - est.
san - na in the high - est.
san - na in the high - est.
rall. al fine
mf

Eucharistic Acclamations

Words: from Common Worship Order One

Music: Margaret Rizza

1.

ALL *mf*

To concluding prayer

Christ has died: Christ is ri-sen: Christ will come a-gain.

mf

Ped.

2.

ALL *mf*

Dy-ing you des-troyed our death, ris-ing you re-

mf

Ped.

To concluding prayer

stored our life: Lord Je-sus, come in glo-ry.

30

3.

ALL *mf*

When we eat this bread____ and drink this cup

we pro-claim your death, Lord Je-sus, un-til you come____ in glo-ry.

To concluding prayer

4.

Lord, by your cross and re-sur-rec-tion

you have set us free. You are the Sa-viour of____ the world.

To concluding prayer

Concluding Prayer

Bles-sing and hon-our and glo-ry and pow-er be yours for e-ver and e-ver.

CELLO (Optional)

DESCANT or MELODY INSTRUMENT

A - - men. A - - men.

A - - men. A - - men.

Great Amen

Words: from Common Worship Order One

Music: Margaret Rizza

Agnus Dei

Words: from Common Worship Order One

Music: Margaret Rizza

Larghetto, flessibile ♩ = c.56-60

MELODY INSTRUMENT (Optional)

mp meditative

mp meditative

rall.

rall.

Ped.
CELLO (Optional)

a tempo

CONGREGATION

mp

rit.

Lamb of God, you take a - way the sin of the world, have mer - cy___ on us, have

CHOIR

mp

S.
A.

Lamb of God, you take a - way the sin of the world, have mer - cy___ on us, have

T.
B.

a tempo

rit.

8
un poco più mosso
mer - cy on us.
MELODY INSTRUMENT (Optional)
mf
S.
A.
mer - cy on us.
T.
B.
Optional 4-bar interlude
mf
11
rit.
a tempo
CONGREGATION mf
Lamb of God, you take a - way the
CHOIR mf
Lamb of God, you take a - way the
mf
rit.
a tempo
mf

sin of the world, have mer-cy on us, have mer-cy on us.

sin of the world, have mer-cy on us, have mer-cy on us.

un poco più mosso

Optional 4-bar interlude
un poco più mosso

20
rit.
a tempo
CONGREGATION mf
rit.
Lamb of God, you take a - way the sin of the world,
CHOIR mf
Lamb of God, you take a - way the sin of the world,
mf
rit.
a tempo
rit.
mf
23
dim.
grant us peace, grant us peace.
dim.
grant us peace, grant us peace.
dim.
dim.

Jesus, Lamb of God

Words: from Common Worship Order One

Music: Margaret Rizza

WOMEN

Je - sus, Lamb of God, have mer - cy, have mer - cy on us.

CHOIR or ALL (Unison)

Je - sus, Lamb of God, have mer - cy, have mer - cy on us.

13 MEN
mf

Je - sus, bear-er of our sins, have mer - cy, have mer-cy on us.

mp

CHOIR or ALL (Unison) al Fine

17 *mf*

S. A.

Je - sus, _____ bear-er of our sins, have mer - cy, have

T. B.

mf

mf

20

f

mer - cy on us. Je - sus, Re-deem-er of the World, have

f

f

mer - - cy, have mer - cy on us. Grant us

peace, grant_____ us peace.

Congregational and Instrumental Parts

Kyrie

Words: from Common Worship Order One

Music: Margaret Rizza

Andante ♩ = c.63-69

Lord, _____ have mer - cy.

Lord, _____ have mer - cy. Christ, _____ have mer - cy.

Christ, _____ have mer - cy. Lord, _____

_____ have mer - cy. Lord, _____ have mer - cy.

Gloria in excelsis

Con spirito ♩ = c.72-76

Glo - ry, glo-ry to God, glo-ry to God in the

high - est, and peace to his peo - ple, peace to his peo-ple on earth.

Lord God, hea-ven-ly King, al - migh - ty God and Fa - ther, we wor-ship you, we give ___ you thanks, we

praise you for your glo - ry. Lord God, hea-ven-ly King, al - migh-ty God and Fa - ther, we wor-ship you, we

give __ you thanks, we praise you for your glo - ry.

Meno mosso ♩ = c.60-66

CONGREGATION (Optional to bar 52)

Lord Je - sus Christ, on - ly Son of the Fa - ther, Lord __ God, __ Lamb of God, you take a - way the

sin of the world: have mer - cy, have mer - cy on us; you are seat-ed at the right hand of the Fa - ther: re-

CONGREGATION

un poco rit. *f*

47

ceive our prayer, re- ceive our prayer.   For

53 **Tempo Primo** ♩. = c.72-76   *f*

you a-lone are the Ho-ly One, you a-lone are the Lord, you a-lone are the Most High,

59   CONGREGATION

you a-lone are the Most High, Je- sus Christ, with the Ho-ly

66   poco rit. *f*   a tempo

Spi- rit, Je- sus Christ, with the Ho-ly Spi- rit, in the glo- ry, the

72

glo- ry of God the Fa- ther, in the glo- ry, the glo- ry of God the

78 *ff*   molto cresc. e rit. al fine

Fa- ther. A- men, a- men, a- men, a- men.

Gospel Acclamation

Con spirito ♩. = c.72-76

MELODY INSTRUMENT (Optional)   If a shorter introduction is required, start in bar 3

CONGREGATION *f*

Al- le- lu- ia, al- le- lu- ia, al- le-

10 **Quasi recitativo**

CANTOR *mf*

-lu- ia, al- le- lu- ia. Example verse: May the Fa- ther of our Lord Je- sus Christ en-

15   rit.   For extended ending cut to

ligh- ten the eyes of our mind, so that we can see what hope his call holds for us.

Simple ending
Tempo I
CONGREGATION
18 *f*   rall.

Al- le- lu- ia, al- le- lu- ia, al- le- lu- ia, al- le- lu- ia.

Extended ending
Tempo I   molto rit. e cresc. al fine
18 *f*   (✓)   (✓)

Al- le- lu- ia, al- le- lu- ia, al- le- lu- ia, al- le- lu- ia, al- le- lu- ia, al- le- lu- ia.

Sanctus and Benedictus

Largo, very flexible ♪ = 116
MELODY INSTRUMENT (Optional)

CONGREGATION *mp*

Ho - ly, Ho - ly, Ho - ly, God of power and might, Ho - ly, Ho - ly, Ho - ly God of power and might,

CONGREGATION *mf*

Hea-ven and earth are full of your glo - ry, are full of your glo - ry.

Ho - san - na, ho - san - na, ho - san - na in the high - est. Ho - san - na, ho - san - na in the high - est.

Tempo I CONGREGATION *mp*

Bles - sed is he who comes, who comes in the name of the Lord. Bles - sed is he who comes, who comes in the name of the Lord.

Ho - san - na, ho - san - na, ho - san - na in the high - est.

Largamente molto rit. **rall. al fine**

Ho - san - na, ho - san - na in the high - est.

Eucharistic Acclamations

Largo ♩ = c.77 ALL *mf*

To concluding prayer

Christ has died: Christ is ri - sen: Christ will come a - gain.

ALL *mf* *To concluding prayer*

Dy - ing, you des-troyed our death, ris - ing, you re - stored our life: Lord Je - sus, come in glo - ry.

ALL *mf* *To concluding prayer*

When we eat this Bread and drink this Cup we pro - claim your death, Lord Je - sus, un - til you come in glo - ry.

To concluding prayer

Lord, by your cross and re - sur - rec - tion you have set us free. You are the Sa - viour of the world.

⊕ Concluding Prayer

f

Bles - sing and hon-our and glo - ry and pow - er be yours for e - ver and e - ver. A - men. A - men.

Great Amen

(♩ = 80)
CONGREGATION

f

A - men, a - men, a - men, a - men.

Agnus Dei

Larghetto, flessibile ♩ = c.56-60
Org.

rall.

a tempo
CONGREGATION
mp

Lamb of God, you take a - way the

un poco più mosso

rit.

Optional 4-bar interlude

sin of the world, have mer - cy__ on us, have mer - cy__ on us.

a tempo
CONGREGATION
mf

rit.

Lamb of God, you take a - way the sin of the world, have__ mer - cy on us, have

rit.

un poco più mosso
Optional 4-bar interlude

rit.

mer - cy on us.

a tempo
CONGREGATION
mf

rit.

dim.

Lamb of God, you take a - way the sin of the world, grant us__ peace, grant__ us peace.

Jesus, Lamb of God

Largo ♩ = c.60
Org.

WOMEN *p*

Je - sus, Lamb of God, have mer - cy, have mer - cy on us.

CHOIR or ALL (Unison)
f

MEN *mf*

Je - sus, Lamb of God, have mer - cy, have mer - cy on us. Je - sus, bear - er of our sins, have mer - cy, have

CHOIR or ALL (Unison) al Fine
mf

< *f*

mer - cy on us. Je - sus,__ bear - er of our sins, have mer - cy, have mer - cy on us. Je - sus, Re -

rit.

Un poco meno mosso rall.
p

dim.

deem - er of the World, have mer - cy, have mer - cy on us. Grant us peace, grant__ us peace.

Words: © Copyright 2000 The Archbishops' Council. Used with permission.
Music: © 2011 The Royal School of Church Music.

C Instrument

Kyrie
Tacet

Gloria in excelsis

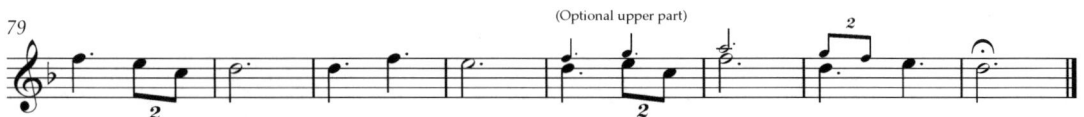

C Instrument

Gospel Acclamation

Con spirito ♩. = c.72-76

If a shorter introduction is required, start in bar 3

Quasi recitativo

CANTOR *mf*

Example verse: May the Fa – ther of our Lord Je – sus Christ en – ligh – ten the eyes of our mind,

rit.

For extended ending cut to ⊕

so that we can see what hope his call holds for us.

Simple ending

Tempo I

rall.

⊕ Extended ending

Tempo I

Sanctus and Benedictus

Largo, very flexible ♪ = 116

Largamente molto rit.

rall. al fine

Music: © 2011 The Royal School of Church Music

C Instrument

Eucharistic Acclamations

Concluding Prayer

Bles - sing and hon - our and glo - ry and pow - er be yours for e - ver and e - ver.

ff ... *fff*

Great Amen

5 (♩ = 80)

f

Agnus Dei

Larghetto, flessibile ♩ = c.56-60 ... rall. ... a tempo

mp *meditative*

7 ... rit. ... un poco più mosso

mf

12 ... rit. ... a tempo ... rit. ... un poco più mosso

f

18 ... rit. ... a tempo

* Optional 4-bar interludes

Jesus, Lamb of God
Tacet

C Instrument

Kyrie
Tacet

Gloria in excelsis

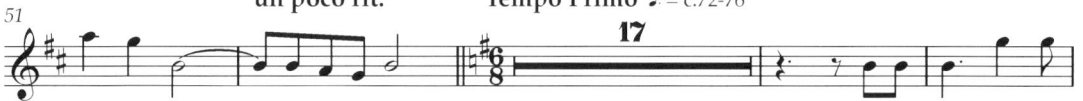

C Instrument

Gospel Acclamation

Con spirito ♩. = c.72-76

If a shorter introduction is required,
start in bar 3

f

Quasi recitativo

CANTOR **mf**

Example verse: May the Fa - ther of our Lord Je - sus Christ en - ligh - ten the eyes of our mind,

rit.

For extended ending cut to ⊕

so that we can see what hope his call holds for us.

Simple ending

Tempo I

rall.

⊕ Extended ending

Tempo I

f

Sanctus and Benedictus

Largo, very flexible ♪ = 116

mp

Largamente molto rit.

f   **f**   **ff**

rall. al fine

C Instrument

Eucharistic Acclamations

Concluding Prayer

Bles - sing and hon - our and glo - ry and pow - er be yours for e - ver and e - ver.

ff   *fff*

Great Amen

(♩ = 80)

f

Agnus Dei

Larghetto, flessibile ♩ = c.56-60   rall.   a tempo

mp meditative

rit.   **un poco più mosso**

mf

rit.   a tempo   rit.   **un poco più mosso**

f

rit.   a tempo

* Optional 4-bar interludes

Jesus, Lamb of God
Tacet

Cello

Kyrie

Gloria in excelsis

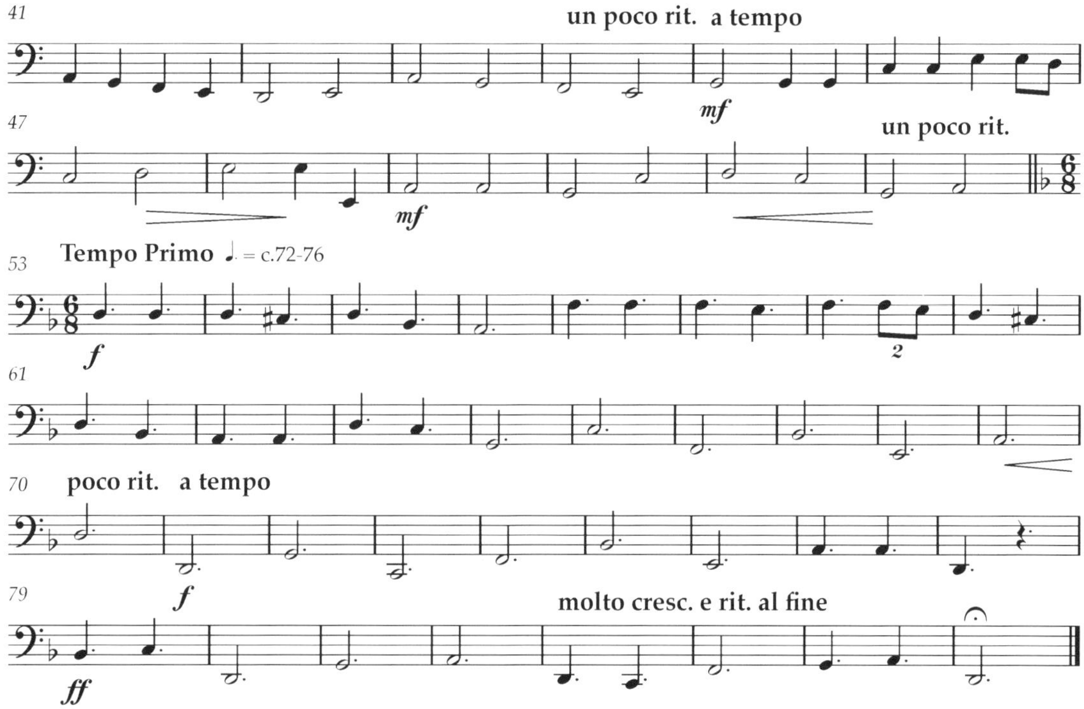

Gospel Acclamation

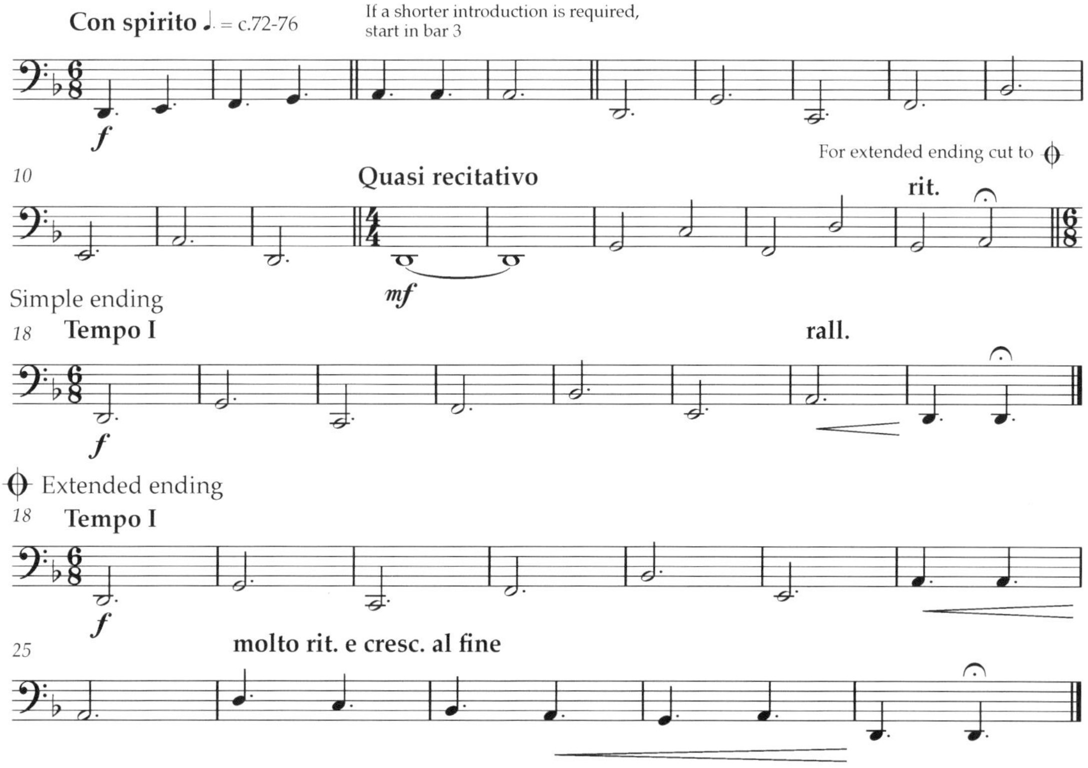

Cello

Sanctus and Benedictus

Largo, very flexible ♪ = 116

Cello

Eucharistic Acclamations

Concluding Prayer

Great Amen

(♩ = 80)   cresc. e rit. al fine

Agnus Dei

Larghetto, flessibile ♩ = c.56-60   rall.   a tempo

mp meditative

7   rit.   un poco più mosso   rit.   a tempo

14   rit.   un poco più mosso

19   rit.   a tempo   rit.

dim.

Cello

Jesus, Lamb of God

Guitar / Vocal part

Guitar / Vocal

Kyrie

Words: from Common Worship Order One

Music: Margaret Rizza

Gloria in excelsis

ceive our__ prayer, re - ceive our__ prayer. For

Tempo Primo ♩. = c.72-76

you a - lone are the Ho - ly One, you__ a - lone are the Lord, you a - lone are the Most___ High,

you__ a - lone are the Most High, Je - sus Christ,___ with the Ho - ly

Spi - rit, Je - sus Christ,___ with the Ho - ly Spi - rit, in the glo - ry, the

glo - ry of God the Fa - ther, in the glo - ry, the glo - ry of God the

Fa - ther. A - men, a - men, a - men, a - men.

Gospel Acclamation

Con spirito ♩. = c.72-76

Al - le - lu - ia, al - le - lu - ia, al - le -

Quasi recitativo

-lu - ia, al - le - lu - ia. May the Fa - ther of our Lord Je - sus Christ en -

For extended ending cut to ⊕

ligh - ten the eyes of our mind, so that we can see what hope his call___ holds for us.

Simple ending
Tempo I

Al - le - lu - ia, al - le - lu - ia, al - le - lu - ia, al - le - lu - ia.

⊕ **Extended ending**
Tempo I — molto rit. e cresc. al fine

Al - le - lu - ia, al - le - lu - ia, al - le - lu - ia, al - le - lu - ia, al - le - lu - ia, al - le - lu - ia.

Sanctus and Benedictus

Guitar / Vocal

Eucharistic Acclamations

Largo ♩ = c.77

To concluding prayer

1. Christ has died: Christ is ri-sen: Christ will come__ a-gain.

2. Dy-ing, you des-troyed our death, ris-ing, you re-stored our life: Lord Je-sus, come_ in glo-ry.

3. When we eat this Bread____ and drink this Cup we pro-claim your death, Lord Je-sus, un-til you come____ in glo-ry.

4. Lord, by your cross and re-sur-rec-tion you have set us free. You are the Sa-viour of____ the world.

Concluding Prayer

Bles-sing and hon-our and glo-ry and pow-er be yours for e-ver and e-ver. A-men. A-men.

Great Amen

(♩ = 80)

A - men, a - men, a - men, a - men.

Agnus Dei

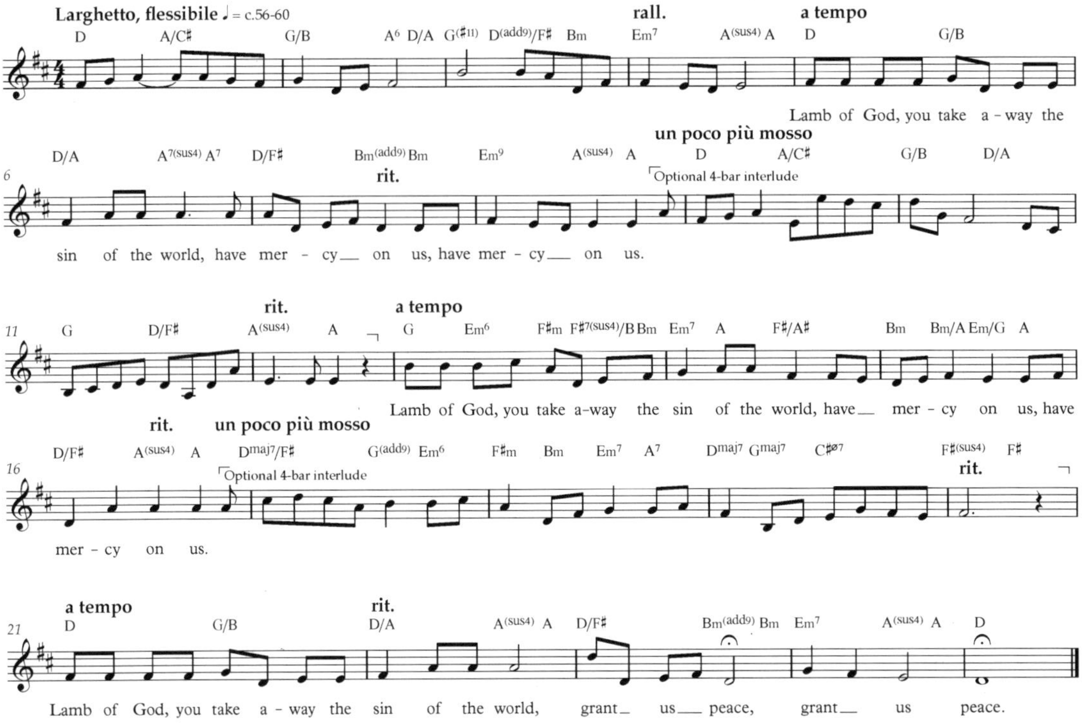

Jesus, Lamb of God

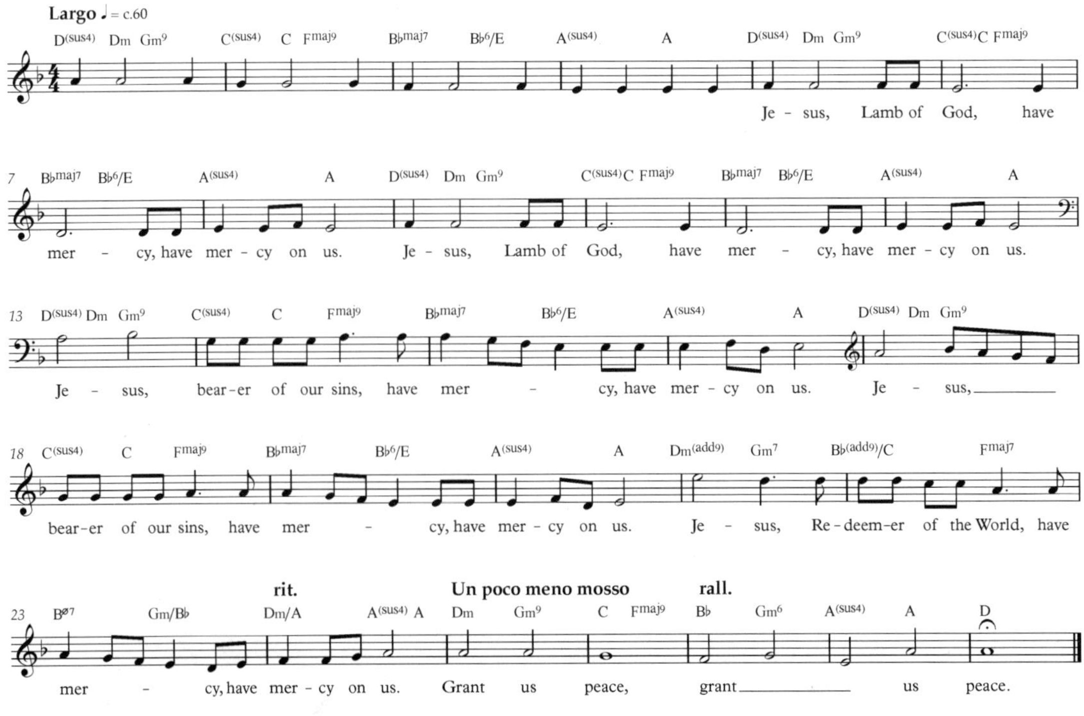